Bitter Words

They can stab you like sharp knives,
Slowly fracturing your mind.
Unpredictable,
They grab you by surprise.
Blowing on your light like a candle,
And taking away the final beat of your heart.

Feeling Lonely

Raindrops running down the window pane,
As if the sky could feel my heartache.
I can only hear the sound of the rain,
Covering the silent emptiness of the room.
When nobody is watching or listening,
What should be relaxing
Makes me feel more lonely.

Wishing you were here.

Desire To Survive

Amandine Chaz

Desire To Survive © 2022

Amandine Chaz

Presentation by *BookLeaf Publishing*

Web: www.bookleafpub.com

E-mail: info@bookleafpub.com

ISBN: 9789357213639

First edition 2022

Childhood

Age of innocence;
Abundance of endless dreams
Robbed in an instant.

Crisis

Cataclysm
Raging in your veins.
Inner fight,
So close to breaking out.
In a merciless environment,
Searching to escape violence.

Panic Attack

It's happening again:
This tightness in my chest,
The struggle to breathe
And feeling like suffocating.

Trembling and sweating,
The world is swallowing me up,
Like an invisible force
That nobody else can see.

I'm paralysed and I'm blind,
I cannot hear a sound.
Only the voice inside my head
And the palpitations of my heart.

But then I feel his arms around me.
His embrace, like a shield,
Protecting me from drowning
Into the depth of my own body.

Anxiety

It's a burden, it's a poison
Spreading in your veins,
Messing up with your brain.
Quiet on the outside,
But so loud on the inside.
Invisible to the stranger's eye,
But so clear and real to the wounded;
Like a dark shadow
Always lurking behind you,
Ready to swallow you up
When vulnerability comes.

Depression

Deeply rooted in our head,
Each thought devouring us.
Praying for it to end,
Relentlessly trying to
Escape from this living hell.
Sleepless nights,
Silently suffering and screaming.
Imprisoned by an invisible demon;
Only left with the feeling of becoming
Numb.

Monsters

The monsters in my head are screaming,
Trying to break free
To take control of my body.

The monsters in my head are uncontrollable.
They spread like a disease,
Looking for any weaknesses.

The monsters in my head are destructive.
Tearing all my limbs apart,
Dangerously reaching for my bleeding heart.

Darkest Hour

I'm looking at this bridge,
Wondering if it's worth the fall.
Would it make the pain go away?
Would it stop my heart from aching?

How can life become so rough?
That it feels like turning into a robot,
With no signs of conscience or emotions,
Just following the master's instructions.

All because your own body tricks you
Into believing
That the world would be a better place
Without you here.

Grieving

I remember the day that I received the call,
The agony that I felt
When they told me you were gone.
All of a sudden,
Everything that we shared was no more.
With a snap of a finger,
You abandoned me here all alone.
I cried, I screamed, I denied it.
I was angry, I was broken, I was bleeding.
But despite the relentless pain,
I know that in the end,
We will see each other again.

Missing You

I can feel this hole in my heart
And tears streaming down my face.
Wondering why the universe
Is keeping you away from me.

Looking at photographs;
It's like the memories are back to life.
But why does it hurt so bad?
Why is fate forcing us to be apart?

If I could,
I would walk for hours,
I would run for miles,
I would climb mountains,
I would swim across oceans;
Only if it meant being with you
So I could stop missing you.

I Wish

12

I wish I had known you better,
To create memories
That would have forged our story.

I wish I had known the man;
The one who had dreams
Ready to be fulfilled.

I wish I had known the father
You used to be,
Not perfect but still trying.

Now all I see are
Tears in my father's eyes,
And a broken heart,
Not ready to say goodbye.

Breathing

Breathing in, breathing out;
The purest ability
Yet, the only one we cannot live without.
Such a powerful sense
Yet, so fragile and precious,
Like a beloved treasure
We're afraid to lose.
It's where life starts
And where it ends.
It's a skill that needs practice
But when you control it,
See the empowerment begins.

Nature Connection

14

Feeling the soil underneath my bare feet,
Touching the bark of a tree,
Smelling the grass after the rain,
Looking around at the top of a mountain.

The blooming rebirth of spring,
The shining light of summer,
The fallen leaves of autumn,
The white cover of winter.

When everybody keeps rushing,
You're the one I always seek comfort in.

Hope

When there's hope, there's light;
The one that we always see
Glowing in the dark.

When there's hope, there's love;
The one that consumes
And rises you above all.

When there's hope, there's life;
The one you've been craving for.
Preserve it.

Stronger

Like a raging fire,
I burned to ashes
My inner demons.
They can try to come back,
But will never reach me.

Like a fortress,
I created a shield
To protect me from my enemies.
Brick by brick,
I built the walls, so tall;
Unbreakable.

Musical Medicine

Music has powers.
It can heal a broken heart
And lift you up from the ground.
Like poetry,
The words can mend your soul,
Allowing you to feel vulnerable.
Music can stop time
And wrap you in an invisible bubble;
The one you never want to burst.
The one who will make you feel at peace.

Power Of Love

To love and being loved:
The most intense feeling on earth.
It can shatter your heart
Into millions of pieces.
But true love can ease
Your inner pain.
It will bring you comfort,
It will be your strength.
On the verge of breaking down,
Love will rescue you,
Like a pair of arms
Holding you up,
And never letting you go.

Survivor

Giving life another chance,
And finally see the light
At the end of the tunnel.

Finding the strength
To pull yourself up from the edge
And break free from the pain.

Reaching for the hand of a stranger,
The one who has always wanted to help
And protected you from your own nightmares.

Walking towards new beginnings;
Fearless and braver,
That's what we call survivors.

Gratitude

20

Kindness of the heart,
Fulfilling and comforting,
Benefits the mind.

Acceptance

At my best or my lowest,
Caring too much and
Craving for attention, but
Evolving to be a better self.
Passionately determined
To create a prosperous future.
Accepting the flaws and
Never doubting myself.
Currently imperfect, but
Eternally at peace with who I am.